In My Absence
Stella Padnos-Shea

This publication is a creative work protected in full by all applicable copyright laws, as well as by misappropriation, trade secret, unfair competition, and other applicable laws. No part of this book may be reproduced or transmitted in any manner without written permission from Winter Goose Publishing, except in the case of brief quotations embodied in critical articles or reviews. All rights reserved.

Winter Goose Publishing
45 Lafayette Road #114
North Hampton, NH 03862

www.wintergoosepublishing.com
Contact Information: info@wintergoosepublishing.com

In My Absence

COPYRIGHT © 2016 by Stella Padnos-Shea

First Edition, August 2016

Cover Design by Winter Goose Publishing
Photograph by Leslie Hendelman-Bliss
1975 Midwestern US lesliehblissphotography@gmail.com
Typesetting by Odyssey Books

ISBN: 978-1-941058-51-0

Published in the United States of America

Contents

Would You?	1
Mama	2
So It's Ours	3
Between Us	4
Love, a Little Bit	5
It Wasn't Light	6
You Must Know	8
Intimate Strangers	9
Eden	10
Necessary Blizzards	11
What Do You Say in an Empty Room?	12
Bad Investment	13
Digits	15
Facebook	16
Read My Lips	17
How to Pee	19
One More Candle	21
Mike Sweats Erin Hard	22
It's a Gift	23
Missing	25
Third Day, Breadloaf; or A Brooklyn Girl Wonders if That's a Bear or a Large Dog	26
Real Barbie	27
Light Is My Daughter	28
Pearl	29
It Started	30
Husbands	32
You In Our Bed	33

Love Worn to Stubs	34
Taj Mahal, USA	35
Fool Me Once	36
Being Dora the Explorer	37
12/29/10	38
Goodnight Stars	39
Brooklyn Wild Cat	40
Third Grade Snapshot, 1978	41
A Small Space	42
Needle's Eye	43
Your Family Grew	44
Streaming	45
Tuesday	46
Language of Light	47
Speed Dating	48
Many Names for Our Parts	49
Automat, 1930s	50
A Day in Room 331	51
Marriage: The Space Between the Betweens	52
Existential Patchy Kit	53
Piece It Together.	54
"Christina wuz here"	55
Losing by Numbers	56
Between the Sheets	57
My Mother Never Taught Me	58
Tumbler	59
Big City Blizzard	60
Looking the Part	61
Advertisement	62
Christ Re-Crucified	63
Layover	64

Tupperware Home Party, 1958	65
Swollen	66
Love Song to Advil	67
Autopsy of the Wedding Gown	68
Holding	69
Urban Hymn	70
Scratchiti	71
You Promised You'd Never Leave Me	72
Groundswell	73
Ana L.	74
Split End	75
Otherwise Known As	76
I Cried for the Places That Don't Exist Any Longer on Your Body	77
Subway Preacher, 6:12 P.M.	78
The Old Way	79
Orchid on Valium	80
Barbie	81
Bubble Yum Woman	82
Crazy Glue	83
Blinded	84
Shore Leave	85
Lovely and Amazing	86
I Remember High School	87
Self-Fertilization	88
The Child Inside Your Mind	90
In My Absence	91
Acknowledgments	93
About the Author	95

To my parents, Evelyn and Norman Padnos

*To coincidence, chance,
and the collective unconscious*

Would You?

He standing, a still life, a lie
that could only apply to him—
skin so static except under his left eye
where the emotion pools,
the face deserted, and I sat.
It was red wine;
it was vodka tonic;
it was Miller Genuine Draft.
He was too cool;
a motion sensor would leave him
in a darkened room for hours.
An apple in the painting
that no one knows how to pick up,
but an edible threat.
It was grey-blue eyes, blue-grey.
A film that got stuck.
He'd leave it on the still; I'd fire the technician.

It was New Year's Eve,
below zero and falling,
next to the water shifting
more slowly than air.
And then you asked—
you couldn't even say my name.
Me standing, you crouching,
us an anonymous, enormous still life.
Even the retriever and his attendant human
slowed down like snow.
Darkness light on our heads, chill heavy below.
Everything light under us,
pushing us up, pushing.
The stars like snowmen rooting for us, pulling.

Mama

I dreamt I was a mother.
(No baby lives in my daytime.)
My child was a dream and so small,
so artificially small,
like a doll for fifty cents
through a vending machine slot.
I kept the baby in my purse
while spending his twilight.
I had to stare hard to see him move,
and this was as subtle
as a change in the eye's glisten.
Sometimes in the middle of being distracted

I'd forget the baby,
and how embarrassing to go into a smoky pub
to ask for an infant.
Once the baby's eyes stewed in strong light
as I looked for my keys.
He didn't blink so I covered his eyes.
I stopped him from seeing the world.
This child does not need me
and I woke up,
bleeding.

So It's Ours

What is life without artificial heat?
We convinced the contractor to keep our walls up—we're introverts—
and instead make his life harder by scooping inside the wall blindly.
He was finding our source. We have just one level. We have no balcony, no second story;
it's all inside our hearts.
The basement is there too; we keep most of who we are tucked behind the eyes.
Especially Daniel with the pale eye crinkled,
like a plastic bag weighted with groceries.
But there's a copper sink,
copper like an Irish girl's hair,
dishwasher as file cabinet,
and small hand-painted tiles
like scattered Bermuda shells.
And so many lack even clean water.
We didn't let him knock down our walls—
that's what marriage is for, if we're lucky.
We have weather only on one side.
We watch it set out there.
Maybe it was easier without Edison's wizardry—
the security of nothing to rely on
but our own shivering.
We still haven't decided how
to handle those walls.
Cobalt blue?
Country peach like a June Friday greenmarket?
For now, still off-white,
the color of an exhausted imagination.
But we're still thinking, and staring at each other, like strangers,
like friends.

Between Us

Inside a box labeled "Drapes and Curtains"
is your black and white face.
The mover had everything reduced
to cardboard boxes.
Your eyes like ripe grapes
peering out of the oval hollow,
where our fingers go.

I can touch the space
your homeless image stares at.
You implicate intimacy so well.
Can we trade backdrops?
I'll watch the photographer
and convince him he is a halo
in the space between us.

Love, a Little Bit

for D.S.

I like you when you're warm,
blanketed in what you won't say.
More beer to peel your cool.
I like that you are
what I don't know.
I miss your aftershave smell of what comes next.
I dreamt about you and woke up
smiling, to see you lie
before my eyes and after.
I linger longer seconds with you.
The dark at night climbs
over your eyes,
in your open mouth,
awake inside your curving arm.
You make my scars more pliable.
You sleep wearing a black mask
to keep the world off your blue eyes.
Blue-grey, you say.
You prefer the sun out of view, a woman bright.
Your arm is the mask I sleep best with,
curling around me like a lifeboat.

It Wasn't Light

It wasn't light that came
to clutch me. It was pain.
Still not yet born,
the last turn you made in my body.

I remember looking down to the bed's edge,
and I saw him, holding an Au Bon Pain paper bag,
that paper bag so still, and there were
lights, doctors, I lay on my right side,
I wanted to tell him I'm fine,
to smooth down that petrified look
like I could untangle matted hair,
but I couldn't speak with oxygen
strapped on my face.
I remember no emotions, no pain,
but his matted, tangled face in fear
and the Au Bon Pain bag growing vine-like
from his hand.

My hospital smock stained with visions
of what was to come. How rude,
how a savior, to put an end
to the delicious agony of your arrival.
You were at my door, pounding,
and I fumbling for the latch.
My hospital frock doused in birds, maybe doves,
I carried soil from your exit for days.
You undid your own burial,
our heartbeats dropped too far,
but you carried puffs of breath,
kicked in them damn walls and haloes,

life was still a stranger
and you were going to meet her.

The doctors yelled at me to push.
I stared at those birds
and someone said they saw black hair.
You took only what you could carry:
breath, heartbeats, sound. You
could not imagine this paradise.

You Must Know

You look at me and don't smile.
You must know I'm evil,
I am not made of pure love for you,
ambivalence is my middle name, or not.
Or you don't look at me as I sing made-up songs,
and you must know my secrets.
What if I am your enemy and I made you,
like a vengeful god.
What if the songs and the nicknames don't matter,
but you know me before the words come out,
like when my body was your home, your unconscious, your heaven.

Intimate Strangers

She brings the blizzard inside.
Her phone number is the weather phone
and she plans her forgetting accordingly.
She sits indoors dripping with outside,
puddles where she goes.
She makes him dance, like rain.

Only what's clear can protect her:
phone booths, the ocean, her own lies.
They walk alone on the shoulder.
She wears dresses with neckline ruffles
to embellish her stories,
the way a storm embroiders the air.

They move south to follow sun without touching.
He returns her father's lighter
which burns a lunar white.
She loosens him of his character,
helping him out of his necktie.

He deals out whispers like cards.
His voice is her invisible atlas.
Each small move reciprocated,
they mimic each other like they're tickling.

Eden

When I saw your flowers,
I knew it was over.
I fell into your colors,
your sticky haloes.
My eyes trapped in amber.
Strands of light braided my clean heart.
When I pried myself from your red,
there was a new hue waiting.
I opened my eyes and smelled orange.

I'd been afraid of love
and its deliberate limbo.
Your curves, your bending into the Earth,
and I lost myself. Thankfully.
I lay on top of you, but I was not like you.
I felt green as your leaves
and could not pick myself up.
Even after my arms grew into wings,
I did not try.
Resting on my two beloveds,
you and the Earth,
I stay and wait,
hoping neither of us can move.

Necessary Blizzards

I dreamt I wasn't faithful; I dreamt I wasn't fair.
Outside people are shoveling what has fallen
so slipping won't occur.
It was a man; a man I didn't know.
A secret being acted out in one room.
Balancing between tears and desire, my face.
This is why we clear the streets:
because it is so easy to go down.
Not one limb at a time; it's one limb,
then the whole body quicksanded,
landing at the feet of a stranger, slowly
making your way up thanks to his grip.

What Do You Say in an Empty Room?

Let's choose the walls we will avoid facing
and what color they will be.
What will we cushion ourselves
from the earth with?
We walk on marble, wood, and linoleum.
Our light comes from plugs and bulbs.
How will we shade the brightness
when we're dark?
I see outside myself clearly through
a spotless window.
I clean and remove all traces of myself.
Do we want our insides out or our outsides in?
A porch with walls?
We have no view.
The coffee table is for cigarettes.
The bookcase is for show.
The luxury of one thing—one color,
one person—everywhere.
What will I share
and what stories are for the attic?
What do we save for never?
How will we present the skin of our lives—
the surroundings that seem so real
until we move out of them?

Bad Investment

The fables and folklore had taught justice, fairness, lack of duplicity.
Judgements easy to make, a scale clearly emerging like on the seesaw.
Seesaws have been re-hauled, vanished from today's playgrounds,
there is too much to go wrong
with weighing our options.
The marriage a bad investment,
but what a special child.
My girl knows a seesaw from songs,
from nursery rhymes,
but she has never sat on one.
We play in different ways,
that is the erosion between grown-ups.
Whiskey double or yoga inversion.
The way we puncture the addict inside ourselves and let her slowly,
elegantly bleed out.
The child, we hope, is a wise investment.
The plotline between the grown-ups thinning, the wife play-acting
with married men in cabs.
Once she caught the eye of the cab driver and the pupils locked
as her nipple was kissed.
The unspoken tongue to the child was always,
Follow your heart's bliss.
Don't let the sacred chatter of your life
turn into a bad investment.
I used to wobble on the seesaw,
the instability threw me.

My eyes locked on the cab driver's eyes
in the rearview mirror,
he was looking back on me.
The news radio chatted in the background.
No one's eyes were on the road,
we were all such grown-ups,
expecting a path would swoon along all our mistakes.

Digits

My mother's hands are a strangling bed,
sheets puddled into corners
with the frame laid bare.
Her fractured lands have always been so:
butter dripping from bone,
softness plucked from metal feathers.
She gathers her feathers and leaves.

One finger can teach a lesson
and remind a full body.
Two fingers pinch a word into its syllables.
Her nails tack my heartstrings.
I re-comb my heart
while she straightens and plaits.
Her hands make ten thousand wings
and one tangled bird.

Facebook

Hung between photos of the children,
the miracle children,
the children crafted with donor eggs,
the children who may one day slay their parents
who crafted them with love and rules and I click on the

footage of one man slaying another.
Shooting, ejecting, again and again,
the opposite of fatherhood.
What are these white mothers teaching
their sons, what are they drinking,
how are they sleeping,
to what devil did they pray
as their bellies grew and
"Ten selfies not to do!" pops in,
shares the screen with the dark dead man,
the man with the blood pooling and

the next link is
"I can't believe it's not butter,"
and I can't believe that to be a human
is only a sinister meaning

Read My Lips

The Coca-Cola bottle offsets her blue nicely.
"Can you hear me?"
he asks. "No, I can't," she answers. She takes the world out of her ears
when she has over-heard.
She examines her clean skin
in a speckled mirror, her eyes without glasses.
She imagines
more than you can imagine.

Lip-reading, as if a face were a page:
something flat to crumple up
and throw away. He starts out
too strong. As he becomes more
feminine, she strengthens. She
doesn't like when he swaggers
towards her,
like he's hungry and mute. She
likes it when she catches him
looking between her breasts, like
he's hungry but afraid to kill the
animal.
She looks at his hands and talks to
his mouth when she's alone.
She wears strappy heels when she
thinks of him. In her deafness,
she knows how to find things. Her
eyes and hands know the other's
moves before they make them.

He keeps his head down when he talks to her
as if he could

sneak into her. As if she will think he's meek,
look away,
and he will pry himself into her many folds.
She keeps overlapping.

Her moment to shine is in her role as mistress. She plays the herself
she wants: sexy and forbidden. Her straight hair begins to curl.
The distance between two places is curving.
Her most sexual moments are when he's mouthing her words.
When he responds to her "slower" and "just right," and her lips
spell the deep inside herself.

How to Pee

They don't tell you
the first time you have to pee after the child comes out,
you will have to page the nurse.
You will press the red button
on the wall behind your bed,
careful to not pull or tangle the IV lodged above your right wrist.
Four minutes later—or a few hours,
you're not sure—
the nurse arrives, who you've never seen before.
She will unplug your IV from the wall behind you,
even though the instructions post
"Do Not Unplug."
She will lead you to the bathroom
and go in with you.
She will show you how to make a solution of warm water
and baby wash
in a squeeze bottle.
She will seat you on the toilet,
as she doesn't trust your legs.
You will then pee, which will sting.
She will show you how to fold the padded bed protector in half, the same
padding that you have been lying on since the child came out,
and in half again,
and lay atop your hospital-grade panties.
On top of this, she will instruct you to add one Securely Yours
sanitary napkin, and then another. You are wearing mesh panties,
which another nurse has wriggled onto your shocked-still

body.
Afterwards, the nurse will squeeze the warm water
and baby wash solution onto yourself.
You will be too worn
to feel embarrassment or pride.
Then you will dab yourself dry and pull up the loaded netting.
Then you flush, wash your hands, and leave the bathroom together.
She will hold you as you walk,
somewhat lopsided you are,
back to the bed, and plug in your IV again.
You will then lie back down, and wait.

One More Candle

I feel old.
I feel older than I've ever been.
I feel like I'm asleep when I'm not,
my face scrawled in sleep lines.
Blame the appearance of age
on the pillow. My body softening,
like shortening, my flesh pressed closer
to the beige waist buttons. The evidence of my life
is starting to become evident,
get called "cute" less,
missing the round hollow of that word.
What to rebel against now that late adolescence,
early adulthood
have distanced themselves in the rearview.
Time to fight myself
like adults do—
eat more pizza,
let the gym membership slide, egg on
the beratement inside my skin.
When the high school girls board the train,
I know the new score.
I am more your mother than you.

Mike Sweats Erin Hard

It wasn't the sterling bath knobs,
it wasn't the re-tooled backyard, the driveway,
it wasn't the upstairs, or the downstairs
which found my jealousy.
It wasn't the second bathroom,
not the organic lavender liquid soap
which nestled in the hearth of my desire.
It was the screensaver on the computer
in the kitchen:
Mike Sweats Erin Hard.
Pregnant with the third child, Erin is
still woman, not vessel,
creator, not captive.
The man is still a man to her.
I'll keep my dust bunnies,
my windows as outdoor space,
the one bathroom for pretend privacy.
But what I wouldn't give for a man around,
and for me to play the only woman.

It's a Gift

It's a gift.
It's a surprise.
It's something you never wanted to open.
A sight you never wanted to see.
You could not have envisioned all those tears inside your body.
How can your body contain itself now,
now that the liquid, the salt water, the ocean laps have bled from your peripheries.
The Mother,
coming home and finding her dead son;
the woman, hearing the gunshot in the next room.
A surprise is not a gift, not a party.
This is the worst day, until your own last day.
Some day, in quite a number of days,
she will find pockets of small gifts, like in an ancient graveyard,
the tombstones like loose teeth
shifting in the spring.
One small gift: she doesn't worry if he's all right
in her sleep.
Another: she is that gritty tombstone, weathered, battered, but standing.
One small day, many days from today,
others will look at her with radiance:
she fucking kept going.
Their eyes will elevate her;
she will be another woman
from today's woman, sobbing face-down
on the pillow.
It's a gift.
It's a nightmare.

It's a tragedy.
It's so many tears, each one a sacrifice
like each blueberry
picked by the migrant worker's bruised fingertips.
To tell her now that it's a gift would be sacrilege.
She would look at you like you've praised demons.
But in a small handful of years, she may believe
that to be a victim is to be a survivor.
That bullet carried a small secret blessing.

Missing

He loves her because her fading has begun.
Her eyes amber in winter and growing gold.
Her neck is the beverage sucked out.
The topography of arms deserting itself,
mountain ranges over rivers.
He loves her so her disappearance will not be shocking,
so when he wakes up and doesn't see her
he will see the pattern of loss:
side view growing crisper,
pupils turning to whites,
the imprint on her pillow harder
and harder to find.

Third Day, Breadloaf; or A Brooklyn Girl Wonders if That's a Bear or a Large Dog

I walk the center of the only road, straddle its solid double line.
I cannot pass myself here.

Clouds parade their Buddha bellies, a little God-plated with light.
Sunset's pink bleeds out like broken yolk.

The Rorschach test of trees turns digital out the window screen,
pixilated shades of green. Two of the trees creak
like the air lies down too hard.

Leaves gossip, scatter themselves
like rumors down the street. The sound is real live static,
an audible marble composition notebook. The tuning forks
of the Earth.

Spiders embroider their own shadow. Worms pirouette
in their newly-webbed home, reclining in silken decay.
The forest is booby-trapped in bands of light.

Kingfishers, so beautiful like most predators.
If you're beautiful, you can eat the living.

I walk into a field, climb onto a rock to call you.
The city's signal releases.
I'm losing you.

Real Barbie

She knows the world will bend to her.
The perfect angle of her arms
holds a tiny eternity which she gives up.

No upside down household for her.
At her most maternal she wears high heels and a baby.
She neatly folds each pile of cheer.

Perhaps she waxes nostalgic for an open end.
Instead she settles for the soft walls of her diorama.
Her body cannot resist vandalism.

There is nothing on the tip of her tongue.
Her eyes are never glassy,
only the shine on her manufactured finger.

Ken dresses her wound with a ring
to heal the hole in her hand.
At last, to be impaled with romance!

Light Is My Daughter

"I don't have children, but light is my daughter."
—James Ensor, on his painting,
Children Dressing, 1886

The small girl he always wanted, the small girl he never had.
He spread her out, or did she do it to herself.
Melting butter for bones, oil slick for feet. No one could bear her,
this devilish dressing on his darkest moments. But the claim remained:
you come from me. I want to be your elder, your founder.
When eyes open, my name on your tongue.

Growing up, she would never stay in one place.
A slippery excuse for a child, she sure knew how to milk it;
dinner at four a.m., skipping lunch to land a spot in the hills
or windowsill.

Where was she this time—
closing his eyes to the image of her feathered eyelashes.
Sometimes she wouldn't show for days, and a shroud fell
over the household. He was knocked
into mourning without her highbeam face. After counting the minutes,
she would return as sudden as she left, like a meteor, that girl.
Opening the front door, suspecting her on the porch, he felt her
before seeing her. His face and fingers warmed. He ran to her,
ready to grab, strike, hold, hold,
but she rose
like fed flames.

Pearl

She knits and makes a man.
Her fingers dance to make his body red.
She pulls him up with needles, with pining.
Eyes closed.
The man in her hands unopened.
He is tight around her clinging fingers
until pierced and looped,
her favorite part.
When she is done,
she will draw him over her,
a blanket or sweater.
He takes her shape.
Her bare body holds him together.
She misses him most in winter, when all she wishes
is for him in her lap like yarn.

It Started

and the end was beginning.
The introvenous was locked into my right arm,
I wore the hospital smock flounced with doves,
my panties were long gone.
At first it was so easy, a cake walk, a drinking game,
the bumps on the screen barely born,
like all of us once.
I just lay back,
yes, I'm fine, honey.
In the middle of the night
the jokes were subsiding,
the abstract enemy of pain
was introducing himself, fast.
The memories go in and out like desire.
I remember climbing onto the hospital bed,
on all fours, and the voice of the kindly nurse,
Baby, you can't be climbin' on the bed like that.
I'll never recognize her face,
and I am long gone for her, as well.
One killer of pain came,
which was not fierce enough.
I'd settle into imaginary sleep
and startle awake,
beginning with a low moan.
I was no different from any other animal then,
a low moan being born from somewhere in my body.
Somehow seconds and hours were passing,
the night was still darkly lit in fabulous Brooklyn.
The gaudy sun was on show when the pain changed;
it was time to push.
A part of my body had to come out,
and I was mistakenly in charge.

Can you believe that the doctor was serious when he said,
I see black hair.
Minutes later, those condensed,
super-real minutes later,
I was handed a person.
This is your open baby from your open body.
It was only the beginning.

Husbands

These are women who marry themselves,
ring fingers with their own names gold-plated.
After the last man has left,
they close their windows like bitter widows,
no more children to call indoors.
They pushed strollers back and forth
like bells that wouldn't stop ringing.
Now they sound each hour when life strikes.
Every day the same
like each apartment in the building stacked up and out,
messy days contained.
The neighbors, the children can't undo them.
No ocean can erase their edge.
They harden into their own men.

You In Our Bed

Tonight, like last night, husband tempted by the couch's quiet:
that plush other woman, slightly concave in the middle
like my body once was, since expanded, shrunk, starved and fed—
Nothing between us but you in our bed.

The most pleasure I've felt has been the absence of pain.
I'd cheat on my husband again with an epidural.
Your debut: messy, requiring containment.
Parts of my body bagged and discarded.
Nothing between us but you in our bed.

Husband's afraid of my body's lower half
and I'm afraid of his fear.
Does a girl have to go back to the hospital to get felt up, pricked?
Nothing between us but you in our bed.

And so, sometimes, it is three in the sack:
Not a kinky college stunt or swapper club
but snoring husband, my wet breast, your mouth, your bobbing head—
Nothing between us but you in our bed.

Love Worn to Stubs

A water of a room.
Toilet continual in the fill.
A tumbler of water in the mouth, down the sides.
Raining the TV, female characters in light, shady borders.
Their definition missing from dictionaries.
When she's excited, her mouth gets wet.
Her far-sighted glasses make eyelashes bigger than the feeling.
Her neck dry, too much to hold.
The tips of her fingernails red, love worn to stubs.
Her boyfriend said, *Why do you watch soap operas?*
They are not you. It is not your life.
She agreed.
But she likes the love stories.
She was a prostitute, but that was six years ago.
Her son looking for her in the street, in motels, under strangers.
Looking at her face, I can't see her.
There is too much on top.
In spandex she hides.
Wears Hard Rock Cafe t-shirts from cities she'll never see.
Now she is afraid of food, of anything that helps.
She won't ask a man for water.
She asks if I'm married, if I share.
I don't.

Taj Mahal, USA

Jersey beach town and its right-on smells: Coppertone, salt, taffy-sugar.
Big-time bets. Cash for gold a block inland where reality is less swept.
High-rollers, low winders. Light dimmed to maximize casino shine,
Miami lip gloss by candlelight. The fainting smell of smoke; addiction starts at the mouth. Cash advance machines loan a future.

I keep sand between my toes. Women bring you drinks, marked up,
but they remember where you're sitting. At Dublin Diamonds.
At Lucky 7s. At Brazilian Beauty, sipping between plastic and ice.
I am re-cast in winning, jackpot lights bouncing off my glasses,
magnified. One more bill, see me, I resemble a jewel.

Fool Me Once

and fuck me twice.
I promise you, lover, I will not feel like a scumbag.
I will not reprimand you—
like the teacher did to my three-year-old.
She stuck out her tongue at another three-year-old;
she is crafting her evolving lies about boundaries;
she is learning her mother's unfortunate tricks.
Fool me once and make up your new name.
We will be low-key trannies together,
all shapeshifting vitalities of our being.
We will huddle together in a tent,
the chilling digits will be our motivation and our curse,
we can play hide-and-seek with our dull, dull day-to-day.
The fool will be me; I will wear the hat and sob in the corner.
Maybe I will find in your body
a new antidote to entertain my moonlit times.
The mistakes keep me,
I keep them like cherished fetuses,
we grow ebullient together.
Maybe I've never met you, or maybe
I've walked through your cigarette smoke
outside the nameless office building,
or maybe I am not real.
I accept the options presented like a gift,
like a submerged treasure.
Who will unearth the next crisis of fun.

Being Dora the Explorer

I am ever-ready, filled over with cheer.
I am not allowed to be alone,
but my absent parents have never told me this.
My best friend is a talking monkey.
You cannot imagine my loneliness.
I am followed by songs of adventure,
even when asleep or having my teeth cleaned.
One day I aspire to an internal monologue.
One day I will yell. I will cry.
I will feel the weight of my fears.

I've been grabbed by a tree.
Enormous snakes have risen from the waters.
And Mama is nowhere near to comfort me.
One day I will read the newspaper;
one day I will visit the slums.
I am living like a tourist trapped in a tower
in a palace-studded town.
I will come crashing down,
either as victim or survivor.

12/29/10

A day off, and I smell like pleasure.
How blessed I am to retain my cartoon button limb
in flesh's center.
Elsewhere in the world,
women walk with their hands extended, their backs bent
like lower case letters.
My hands are begging on myself, equal in needs and pleasure,
naked. The shackles of taboo melt when I touch them,
when I drag the text out from under the bed.

Goodnight Stars

"Goodnight stars goodnight air."
I read to my baby on my lap and the words sound final,
sound infinite, like the choice to jump, to fall from Earth.
Was this what you thought—goodnight air, breath going stale,
goodbye. You were closing, you were closed, something was already
slammed quite shut for you. But this baby, my baby, is so open,
she cries and laughs with such ease.
We place her gentle, delicate in her crib, and she falls into
something each night she cannot name.
Waking used to frighten her terribly,
she had just been somewhere else, and now her eyes open
onto light, onto my eyes, and I am smiling.

Not you, you were so crushed, planning your bloody escape,
"goodnight noises everywhere."
My baby, this baby, I hope would never understand such pain,
that she could whisper goodnight to the world.
She's a baby, as long as I'm here, her world is.
"Goodnight to the old lady whispering 'hush'." When you
died, I wanted to make a baby from your dead body,
I was that desperate for life;
can you even imagine that,
John?

(Excerpts from *Goodnight Moon*, by Margaret Wise Brown, 1947)

Brooklyn Wild Cat

I told my girl, *You've got a bad case of saucy face.*
But she claimed
No, no!
when my hand with the grasped napkin
moved toward her mouth.
She wanted the stain,
she wanted the spaghetti sauce
as disguise on her clean white skin.
Who is she, really—
a feral child,
a small hunter in the wilds of Brooklyn?
She is the girl wearing a masquerade of bloody face.
And me, with the nerve, the mindless culture,
to try to groom her into what,
a lady?
She knows to nurture that wolf-girl.
Not even my own mother,
the layers of lineage,
could remove her wildness.
If that spaghetti sauce,
if that blood of the defenseless tomato
is ever to come clean, it will be her tongue
to preen those whiskers.

Third Grade Snapshot, 1978

I pull your childhood from my wallet,
a nine-year-old face stuck among my twenties.
Open during the flash, your eyes snuffed the light.
They match the manufactured sky
over your shoulders.
A mistake to try to decipher them;
they answer like sky or water and repeat the blue.
Better to look for your thinnest skin, under the left eye,
where the dirty laundry of feeling piles up.
Your teeth glisten.

Such a small boy, already boxed in
by one man's view.
It's easier to smile at a stranger.
At home, you preferred the smiling cube of your room,
outside of father's glare.
Who is your mother—
the photographer, more pleased
with a smiling boy?
The only one to record you and make you real?

Close the decades easy as a wallet: back in my pocket.

A Small Space

Between the backseats, a car seat, a small space designed to secure
the product of our sex, a small space where we store our unspokens,
and our expressions of sing-songy glee. The resentment
will have to wait in the back seat of our voices,
Can you hear it, darling?
We don't sleep. We speak to the car seat, to the adored flesh strapped
into its safety and monotony, we ask,
Where is the apple?
Between the voices we assume something else lives, or lived.
A hum, a static that still flickers when we turn out lights,
when the dark comes on. I had a body before this baby.
Do you remember this small space,
my darkness?

Needle's Eye

Beside him
everyone dims.
Not one moment
flickers.
He multiplies
himself by silver:
inside an elevator,
he is a drop
of mercury that rises
and falls,
one slipping detail.
In a cracked windshield,
his seams show
in each glass sliver.
Shadows make
his length alive.
A car breaks through
twilight's pewter web.
It stitches itself
into the sweater
of the city,
as silver loops
through his lobe.
He applies dusk
to his body,
still as moonlit granite.
The mirror tips,
spilling himself
everywhere.

Your Family Grew

like broken yolk while I was away,
like a long, elusive joke. I couldn't smile for you.
The trees shake and shake and spread their seeds.
In the shade, on the ground, a sweet boy
takes off his glasses before he speaks.
Straddling the curb of adolescence,
he already knows that talk
is cheaper than thought.

Oh my God. And I'm in love with him
in a whole new way. I want to touch his hair
as if to comfort him,
to kiss his forehead like I can smooth his thoughts.
I don't want to take him to bed.
I don't want to excite him.
I want to make him a more peaceful boy.
I want him to be my son.

Streaming

Turn on Tavern on the Green
Christmas trees, each branch streamed in light like
a girl radiating, each finger prickling heat-wise
and my words which stream past my father's
hearing-aided ear like a downhill sliding child
(my words a sliding child past my father)
The slowness of sound is infinite
(the infinite slowness of sound to my father)
His ears lit only by evening
the voluptuous awakening of night in his ear
My words fleeing before spoken
like fairies before dawn
The girlish corpse of sound in his ear
(his ear is sound's funeral)

Tuesday

So-and-so washes her hair twice weekly, if a special occasion calls for it.
Mostly she prefers hair powder, baby powder, the addition of gels,
mousses, gelees, applied with the utmost un-care to amplify a look
of styled decay. That is how she would describe her mother
if someone asked, but only to herself in her innermost monologues,
the ones so intimate that they are not even monologues,
but mostly wordless floating ideas, pillow-like silvery things
she can rest her head into after a long day. So many long days.
Walking home from work after the train to the bus to the bodega
for two turkey and American cheese sandwiches,
extra mayo for softness.

Ma calls. So-and-so knows it's Ma not so much from the ring,
not from the time of day, but from the quick quiet
after the answering machine picks up, the
"I'm not home right now, so please leave a message,"
beep, then the gathering of breath to talk, the peace of Ma
sucking the air. "So-and-so, pick up the phone. I know you're home.
I have some new things for you—you know, old things. Pick up, baby."
But not today, knows So-and-so. Today I'm alone, she wants.
Going to start a new biography, someone else's,
the last was George Hamilton's, his teeth more lustrous
than the marooned velvet draped behind him.

Language of Light

The whiteness, my opaqueness had blanketed me
in a language of light, not fury.
One to four.
Two to six.
Three to nine.
I and my young child,
the girl who cannot undrape the veil of white,
her eyes of translucence,
think numbers, think marbles, think hours of daylight.
The sixteen-year-old boy encased in luminous onyx
knows the leaden death of exiled years.
He says—I caught that record when I was eleven.
He says—I didn't even have a suit for trial.
He says—I don't know what my last name really is.

Speed Dating

The woman lifts her hand to her heart,
patting its hard work.
She loads her ashtray in a slow burn of double meaning:
souvenir, absence.
Her mouth open in a loose-fitting curl
pinned all night.
What is her mouth open for?
What is about to enter her.
She is receiving; she is a receipt.
She is itemized and rain checked.
She is standing in line, marketing her brand. No-nonsense.

A shining ruby mouth is an appeal, an advertisement,
a question.
Diamonds revolving the finger a promise, an arrangement,
a hurry.
She has only her mouth strained open, stained a bleeding
color.

Her hands clasped in her lap like a store-bought bow.
Her mouth chewing on its straitjacket
as she pulls out wishes like bunnies: suburbs, teacups,
porcelain.
Her body stands guard against break-in; her laugh the alarm,
three a.m. blaring. Nobody falls asleep
to the sound.

Many Names for Our Parts

Many names for our parts: "wound," "hole," and juicier than those.
The hole was the center of my body, a small child was coming out,
making her exit, making her entrance.
Pushing through the wound of my body, pushing through days and days.
I could not believe that there would ever be an ending,
likely I would be lying on the makeshift bed for years.
I had come to accept this when cries came, someone else's.
You are crossing so many lines, sweetheart,
from unborn to alive, from pain to stillness.
Everything was soaked with meaning.
I can still feel it now, miles of heat scrambling towards me.
The day my body became a gaping wound,
an unimaginable Eden,
a den of fear and sin.
We didn't know what to call her—
let's just call her "Sophia" and be done with it.
But instead our papers named her "No Name Shea,"
and we made our exit.
She is "Mirabel," a name that captures, at best, half-truth,
like "wound" or "hole."
What is caught inside that plumber's locker—
I bet that holds some secrets you'd have to pry out of dead hands.

In My Absence

Automat, 1930s

A simple time, when plans could work. The future tucked
behind a translucent door, the opposite of a game show.
You didn't have to guess Door #1, 2, or 3 for your prize,
then go home a laughing stock with a toaster
when the brand new car was next door. Three coins in the slot,
open the door, lunchtime. A life like that, perfect and unimaginable,
you can almost hear the TV theme song singing your simplicity.

Marry that boy across the street in the window, make it
so that he will choose you, like you're the best sandwich that day.
He'd better be hungry so he wants you. He will open your father's door
and you'll be on the sofa, preened and ready to be taken in.
Lunch was settled with pocket change; what will be your fee?
Everything labeled just so, sandwiches, sandwiches,
cakes, pies, suburbs. Sometimes it hurts to see what you're getting into,
those windows so clean. The wife's job:
to keep things clear and thoughtless.

I'd be the one stuck, tuna fish or grilled cheese?
Tuna fish or grilled cheese? Standing there, starving,
while others have the good sense to know what they want
and pay for it.
BLT, easy come easy go, they're not trying to lose a lifetime
imagining an imaginary choice.

50 Stella Padnos-Shea

A Day in Room 331

Time is first to go.
The clock face turns
featureless. Everyone stares at TV static
like it's the afterlife. Peter
may some day be able to eat a very small thing
like pudding or a tiny sandwich.
He cannot be seen except by family.
To others he is a reminder they would rather see fade

into an ash or jaundice color.
His wife cannot tell if he understands her
after thirty-seven years together.
Overlooked moments are stacked
like regrets. A whisper
is raised to her ears.
It could be from above.
She held his hand for eleven hours

without any of him knowing.
They took turns feeling like plastic. Peter
has a small paper icon taped to his bed.
Its erosion reminds us of the eternal.
His wife gave the nurse her travel icon
while she was gone one hour to eat a very small thing
like pudding or a tiny sandwich.

Marriage: The Space Between the Betweens

I wonder what he's thinking.
Does he know the answer.
Can he read the broken novel in my eyes.

His pillow rests slightly on top of mine. Crowding my thoughts.
Or stealing. Sometimes I pretend to be sleeping alone.
I hear a slow moan as he sleeps, our canyon's tour guide.

Do we need separate sinks. So our germs don't mingle.
We enter or close each other, doors with a trick lock.
Which side am I on.

Who crosses, who stands ground,
who wants more.
Our frayed edges suggest desire.

We speak the same language,
deciphering our silence.

A ceremonial *you* on the tongue's tip
as we pledged instant infinity.
Wars start real small.

Existential Patchy Kit

His death: a temporary eventuality.
While mourning is our tyrant, his cracks are sealed,
his holes filled. We are starting to go under.
His context changes. A breath glows: his?
I am begging.
The big bang all over again, but personal.

Gutted and renovated.
A car battery fused into an alarm clock;
this energy beyond flicks and vibes.
I imagine him re-imagined:
triggered, re-vamped.
A stranger will be born, one step closer
to full repair. We will never meet.
And it will be him.

Piece It Together.

That is the trick, that is the salvation.
To make the life, to make the death, a story.
Use that contrary devil mind to create one pair of eyes upon your time.
Me? I hope I'm only half-way through, or less.
I read today that 95% of your worst experience
can become your best teacher.
Well. When I found the dead body,
not even make-believe God himself,
that sinister Santa Claus with his "naughty" and "nice" lists,
could've told me that shit would work out.
But, with John dead,
we were free to make a new unimaginable,
and unimagined, person,
my Mirabel.
She is the siren blaring down the highway of my life.
I have no narrative but her.
She is smart enough and fool enough
to believe the world is hers.
She has a pretend friend named "Yo-Yo" who she defines.
"This is hard for me, but I can do it."
"Mommy, you're a funny lady."
She doesn't know anything about me, really, except my name, Mommy.
No doubt she will be wiser and taller than me.
She doesn't know that I want to escape her love sometimes.
I hide that from her.
God must know, too, that we are terrified of such a wild love.
That must be God's story, such loneliness.

"Christina wuz here"

she scratches her chalk on pavement.
Sixteen letters, sixteen years
cling to earth's rough surface.
Her name will last as long as the fidgeting sky.
The chalk lingers loosely
when she feels like crumbling.

Her name remains after she walks away.
With so much up in the air,
she finds her weightless footing
as Christina in color, a sidewalk celebrity.
Her name in baby blue
before she becomes where she's headed:
Christina in dust.

Losing by Numbers

Speak in figure eights.
You're far apart and return
to my peeling heart.

Quality of life
falls while you rise unattached,
your sirens blazing.

In your chair I place
phone books from distant cities.
I can't sit alone.

A pile of matches,
a stack of transformations
waiting for one strike.

Christmas without you:
Unravel light. Plug it in.
Decorations done.

In ecstatic ash
you are younger than ever,
time your only crease.

Between the Sheets

I no longer know how to take you.
I no longer know how to hurt you.
This is why we are ending, fading,
the last of the fireworks sliding away in smoke,
the nighttime black reclaiming.
Between the sheets we are apart,
like nighttime stars, years and years of light apart.
We don't collide, we don't coincide,
there is no light, no dark between us.
There is absence. That is what we are living in.
I wonder when our girl will notice that the love
leads only to her, away from the two
who love only her. I lie
above the sheets, thinking of old loves while you sleep.
How did we spend our time, now that we two are spent?
Between the sheets lie games.
Our girl plays peek-a-boo between the sheets,
and she laughs wildly.
Three years old,
and already she knows the delight in being found.
At the joy in another's face in seizing her.
When did we fail each other, but, of course,
it wasn't just one day.
It is, it has been, a series of errors, of choices
to un-love the other.
I no longer stray between the sheets with you.
I am on top, careful to peel, to separate, in all small ways.
Peek-a-boo, you never even knew
I was here.

My Mother Never Taught Me

I pray my girl will say, will spew to those with the nerve to listen
to a nervy blonde, blue-eyed child-woman.
I am "mother" in that sentence. I am good enough at the world
that I want her to be herself. I was just telling Gigi that my girl,
my two-and-a-half-year-old girl, tells me with regularity that
"I do not love you, Mommy." Well. "Maybe tomorrow," I say,
"we'll check back in." She hammers the floor with her child-tools
and loves her stuffed "lamby" so well. Maybe I am teaching her
about love, that she doesn't have to earn me.
She looks into her lamby's glass eyes, rolled off some assembly line
deep in China by perhaps unloved, uncared-for worker-children.
"Are you all right, lamby?" she asks. "Lamby says he is all right."
She is teaching herself goodness; she is showing this shape
of fake animal what kindness means. She will stare into the face
of anyone; she taught herself that curiosity means love.
The subway preacher singled her out once—
"The only person who can look at me is that baby.
When she dies, she will go to heaven, she is just a pure baby."
I didn't know how to teach her on that Q train, we just sat,
mesmerized, watched, and listened.
And I am teaching her that that is enough.

Tumbler

A mother sees me and instantly
congeals into place, moves me towards center.
An adolescent boy likes that I am like him,
pushing my luck, asking for touch without asking.
He drives too fast, too late, what is he asking for?
Small girls like to look through me,
find comfort in seeing a spoon bent by water. One girl's angular body
breaks light into rainbows in dreams.
The father doesn't care. He picks up the glass,
who drank my juice? Pulp still clinging
at the table's edge. No one touches the danger.
Mother loves the state of almost,
walks off. Girl looks for prisms in her fingers.

Big City Blizzard

What is the difference between trapped and enclosed?
Sheltered or victim. Words that lead to war.
I am enclosed because I believe I will be able to leave,
when the weather is ready by my standards. American standards.
Standards as white as the air moving outside my blue window,
someone hired to paint it blue.
Is the young bride trapped or enclosed in white, an iced look
as she flips the switch in her eyes at the altar.

The confidence in being able to leave: this means freedom.
The mayor, who I did not elect, has advised us to stay home.
I do not anticipate being shot if I go outside,
unlike other parts of town.
This has nothing to do with weather, but with white.
White is moving horizontal outside my window.
The wind believes in destination.
The fire is kept inside where it can be adjusted.
We are glued to our TV sets of plasma, watching them measure
and organize our white.

Looking the Part

Enveloped in disguise, serene in her blue gauze of lies,
his green gaze of mischief.
Looking at the part where the steady unspooling began, it was precisely
when her body became apart, began to open, to concede another human,
their human. It was so easy now to fix the gaze on her,
the infantile one, and she felt the grey cloud of being glanced past.

She felt lonely inside all that need.
Stranded inside the absence of desire.

Looking the part of Mother horrified her with pride. How many days
had she forgotten to brush her teeth, to care for the skin and bones
draped on her psyche. The child was a beauty—
Are you the nanny? they would ask. *I am her mother*,
a hard smooth stone in her throat. She looked the part of someone
living in necessity, without adoration and adornment.
Perhaps she could look the part of foolishness, or vixen, or bad decision.
She could unwrap the oversize plaid flannel
and apply something red, something inviting disaster. A little number
that would have to be peeled free. What if she needed
to be cut out of the wreck like that,
one small mother panicked inside the crushed foreign metal.

Advertisement

Prophet has power to help charmed ones deal with unnatural conditions.
One visit will convince you. She is true born.
She can remove love,
will reunite separated feelings.
Lost nature?
She can read your entire life without asking a single question.

Time and distance are no object.
She will remove all spells in less than one hour,
guaranteed.
Twenty-one years' experience in love and court cases.
She keeps her promises.

New solution for an old problem:
Stop washing it in salt water solution.
Your tears are not new.
They have cleansed the problem daily and made it shiny.
Put your tears back inside.
Your problem will grow old and forgetful
with so little attention and preening.
The problem will die and you will have many good years left.

If solution changes color or becomes cloudy, do not use.

Christ Re-Crucified

Christ re-crucified, I read as Christ re-cuperated.
All the names, paraphrased, that have been affixed to your holiness,
to your holier-than-thou-ness, but it is your disciples who put on airs.
You seemed quite down-to-earth, imminently of this world.
Even a woman bore you, cleaned you, nursed you from her body.
Mama Mary sung to you from her pillow book,
praying you would doze

for an hour or two, so she could grab some shut-eye
and rest her thoughts in lilies and afterlife.
But for now, she was your captive, that is to say, your mother.
Your prisoner of grace, while you babbled her body home.
At four a.m. on a handful of sporadic hours' sleep, every mood is the dark side of the street.
You knew to seek her face in times of fear, of fretting, of hunger.
She carried you, she made you, until the end of home,
when you became a widow to nurturing. You no longer needed need.
Even the sponge lightly dipped in wine, raised to your bruised lips
on the cross, was merely gravy, wasn't it?
You had an "in," your dad couldn't just make the call,
your dad was the call.
I guess we'll call it sleep for the next few days, followed by levitation
and high wires.
Please do pay due consideration to our needs;
we are a shyly desperate bunch.

Layover

House me like your body is an airport,
where I can be no where, in no city,
estranged from deity,
my legs stretched between arrivals and departures.
All I can do is to climb your cuticles, pace back and forth
along your limbs.
You share with me your trinkets, so that I may recollect
my days of nowhere.
I may be able to place my fingers on the mouth of a
keychain,
or along the hard edge
of a bookmark, and remember the spaces where our bodies
pressed,
like between the pages of a bullshit romance novel,
where the only feeling is desire, and then more.
That is what I want, to be bookmarked between those two
pages,
between those two legs of the journey:
desire, and then more than that.

Tupperware Home Party, 1958

We are sitting in a circle, we are white, smiling and clean,
like the mouths of the Tupperware bowls we celebrate.
The woman at the center opens a lid, or is she closing it,
what is her relationship to chaos, is she willing to become
unleashed?
We are sitting, hands in our laps, clasped, thighs pressed
as if our seats are crowded, as if we're saving room,
as if we're luggage overpacked and are about to rupture.
Speak to us, Tupperware Leader,
of what we can store in a white plastic shell.
You will tell me how to set my hair in rollers,
perhaps using bottle-shaped containers.
Everything will be just so, oh won't it?

There is a mural behind us,
an expansive image of trees and grass and shade.
Have I misplaced something in these woods?
I keep turning my head to see behind me.
I bet I could lay something down in that made-up grass
and no one would find it but me; no one would know to
look.
Say, a key or a dime or my interior life,
the part that leaves me when I awaken.
A part of me that is too small or too large
for these Tupperware containers,
something I would not be serving my husband as leftovers on
Thursday.
I have never realized my loneliness, Mrs. Tupperware Leader,
until I arrived to your Sarasota home, a lovely living room it
was.

Swollen

She stored every scrap in her body:
this secret between ribs, that trauma in a toe bone.
On went years of perfection, long polished fingernails at a good job.
The prevalence of surface.
She thought her disguise fit better,
pushing each weakness deeper and downer
until she had them buried under years, under skin.
But they were gathering strength while she slept.
The souvenirs began to turn on her,
stain seeping from the inside out.
Her bones hurt; her fictions became fevers.
Incurable memories multiplied inside her.
She needed transplants from people who spoke their stories.
Voice becoming medicine,
poison evaporating like an echo.
Her truth became a tumor that wouldn't stop growing.

Love Song to Advil

I did not know, I'd tried for so long not to touch you
They say you slowly weaken me, make me less of myself
That sounds like the day-to-day ritual of love
my wanting, my fearing
you touch me where I cannot feel it, and everywhere
O Advil: you make all those bullshit metaphors come true
How do you find my pain?
Just one small circle, like swallowing a wedding band
a promise of forever, a waterfall of tomorrows, one by one
One circle, you've found me from my insides out,
you've figured me
you've cured me
Soon we will both dissolve,
the very definition of ecstasy

Autopsy of the Wedding Gown

unzip your cover/flesh
inspect
in a body bag

lying face-up on the dining room table
chemicals to preserve you
in years I may unearth you and expect no smell

look at what covers the body
then go deeper
you have to be ready for the wake

I'm sorry,
wedding—
when I wear you

when I put your skin over mine
make us look like our old selves
it's uncomfortable to wear

this extra layer/skin
people stare
choosing their favorite flaw

they expect me to look half dead and fully made up
but I lie
secure in my peeling

Holding

"Don't hold on to me," Jesus said to Mary like he was too light,
heavy light dark in her eyes and pouring past her.
She tried to hold out her hands but the light left a burn, the heat
from not holding. The air felt hot even without his hands.
Look how lonely your world is without my turning around it.

And she recreated whole rooms of belief in her head:
the instant stained glass her house wore. Her mind traveling further from home. He said
and so I don't give you bows or roses but my blood and bones.
But she is the one who turns blood into children.

Urban Hymn

His eyes closed, sight so absent that the lids can flicker
like his dream is a breeze,
and after minutes, minutes that hold hours of dreams
like this subway car clutches us in its tarnished heart,
his head droops
like a slinky teen sneaking down the stairs past midnight.
He nods a lopsided *yes* onto her shoulder, split paperback in
her lap.

The urban lullaby continues like breath in the chest,
rising on the bridge,
the local lowering under ground.
A silver thread weaves through the city.
And still his head brushes her coat,
her eyes narrowing on the words between her hands.
She doesn't move; she's living in her own story.

When we're most exhausted, we lean into what might not be
there,
and hope the emptiness, or a stranger,
will catch us.

Scratchiti

His key
ekes out initials
on Lucite.
On the long local
back to Mama's,
it opens
a new person,
smoothly as a moving platform.
He spells
his mask out.
His breath speaks.
If he lived in town
he wouldn't have time
for such fame;
he could walk home,
take a cab or a bus.
But on this sixteen-stop ride
he can care
for his name,
and disfigure the window
on the city he hates to love.
Concentric anger in the circle
above the "I,"
a memento
that won't heal.
A family eats dinner
inside the triangle of his "V."
He looks into homes
through the holes
in his name.

You Promised You'd Never Leave Me

your eyes smooth and serious, but it wasn't your death
that made you a liar, it was me, my memory letting go of you
in small steps, first your teeth,
then your fingernails,
your toes,
my mind outliving its desires as yours did, the places
where your body ended a mirage caused by my heat
meeting your cold eroding body, so I can see your knee
clearly
with an indented scar but my memory
ends at your ankles

Groundswell

The calm green land is repeating,
the way a dreaming girl rolls back and forth in her bed.
Her hand touches

her body's bark and peaks like wings touch air.
You'd think she was waving goodbye to someone loved.
The earth murmurs. Pupils widening like thighs.
The girl's long hair waves hello across her pillow.

Her eyelids roll like rolling hills,
dreaming under the lid.
Girl after girl rolls down the same hill,
laughter rising like grass.
Girls' eyes trace their earthen profiles,
compressed quakes pressed into their palms.

Ana L.

He made her strip, remove everything,
to inspect her flesh, root to tip.
Pore over every pore expecting evidence
of other men.
The last time he grabbed her by the neck, she dropped her
mistake of showing fear.
Instead she grabbed him right back and clenched,
through her teeth, "I can squeeze just as hard,"
and he let go.
She admitted to the relief when he hung himself.
When she goes out for laundry, a star twinkles.
It is laughing into her eyes. She is comforted,
then cries.
His gift was magic, a disappearance.
She doesn't wake up to his pacing with a knife.
The fingerprints around her neck are unpeeling, swirl by
swirl.
After all the booze, she muses,
maybe he just fell asleep in that noose.

Split End

"Sometimes at the end things break apart,"
Mama said,
unwinding my staircases of braids.
She'd try to climb into my thoughts this way, through tangles,
her fingers spooling my small voice.
She eyed the end of a brown strand, where one hair became two.
My hair spiraled still into the air.
"Don't pull," I pressed, keeping my worries under her fingers.

She wasn't talking about split ends,
but about my father:
no amount of care could keep
a dead thing together.
And with her eyes on the soft sweep
of what fell to the floor,
Mama started to cut.

Otherwise Known As

This marriage, otherwise known as this union,
this life sentence.
This pairing of husband and wife, for better or worse,
for richer or poorer,
living in the lack of agreement, we can agree
that we are spiritually spending,
expending, the other.
We, otherwise known as x and y, also known as
x or y. Neither x nor y.
One or the other. Neither.
We are a dangling clause. An imperfect participle.
We prefer our pronouns separate, thank you.
Me or you, otherwise known as,
there have been lovely times.
Hey, remember when, and the voices trail off.
It was a startled look on our faces when we were first pronounced.
When we were claimed "husband and wife."
I was now another, expected my name to fade with a replacement ready,
my father delivering me to slaughter. Rhymes with daughter.
The men give away, and the men take possession.
I, in the photo remnants, fare slightly better than cattle,
I am being delivered to a particular bidder.
None of this is completely true, but I was being walked down the aisle into
an imaginary future.
But we do this every day,
walking ourselves into a best guess.
At best.

I Cried for the Places That Don't Exist Any Longer on Your Body

the veins that have been bulldozed by larva,
peaks and tunnels where my lips had landed
dusted away like prints.
Shops where we strolled,
bought cheap flannel pajamas,
now doomed like our time.
I cry when I come.
The glistening vibrator doesn't know my name,
never held my hand on the bed while we both lay there in silence.
We had everything left to say, didn't we.

Subway Preacher, 6:12 P.M.

The edges of her pocket bible worn,
but you should see those words,
worked over like that crop was feeding a nation.

The Old Way

There were no trees
There were no men
There was no length
There was no anger
There was no war
We held court in the late mornings, after jasmine tea, cooled enough
to drink through bendy straws
There were petty disagreements, escalating as the moon waxed
There was roughage, there was grass, shrubbery, walnut pancakes
We played cards, we ran for sport, we had no destination
Our bellies no longer turned full, we stayed to ourselves when we saw fit

I opened a stand on the balcony and sold trinkets
I knew no one would visit my worn merchandise
I saw no end result from my actions
I wanted a return to conflict
I wanted to press against something or someone who would alternately
love and shame me
I wanted to gnaw at the bone of a killed animal
I wanted a return to the old way
I wanted to stop talking, stop dissecting each emotion
I wanted back each delicious mistake, to be relived on my deathbed
I wanted to primp and wax and argue with myself
No one could provide me with the answer to my needs
Every mirror had been broken;
we knew what we looked like by the expression on the passers-by faces

Orchid on Valium
for J.F.

All the unseen communication had disappeared.
We were left with just the obvious.
The computer wouldn't tell us
the weather. I assumed we could look outside.
In lieu of digital distraction, you offered you:
A hug.
Yes.
You found me. Not a word.
I went further into myself with affection,
self-imagining as an orchid on Valium.
Serenely electric.
I wasn't done when the hug was.
I used to be the young one, Jenny.
Now your wet eyes, like globes,
are telling me I'm right here.

Barbie

No matter what form your body takes.
Your mouth is a gaping jar of air, eyes half aloof.
No tongue to slow you with speech or kissing.
Fingertips to never print your memories.
A halo of fingers in protest.
You need more hands to make up for lack of sense.
Your pelvis is most bendable, feet a smudge, mind stilled out.
A self is its surface, no frame remaining, a chrysalis in a firm case.
You are in prom light, time knocking on the outside.
As life falls through my fingers, you collect it on your eyes, dusty but easily cleaned.
Barbie, carry me across these minutes into your puddled lips, into the dismembered heaven of your body.
Curl the ends of my story as perfectly as your hair.
Lather, rinse, repeat.
I want to rest my head in your coma.

Bubble Yum Woman

Wintermint gum is in
a chewing woman.
Friendships have lapsed as space will;
family is distant as time does.
The gum is reckless
and tickled by teeth;
the woman laughs with her friend.
Strangers are flavors
of sticks or chunks.
The woman knows personalities
of pieces per chew.
Cheeks bloom for bubble-blowing
and the hollow of without.
Sometimes the gum is instantly stale:
a sign of gum's sadness
and the woman's face will sag
like wrappers unravelling
over piece
by piece.

Crazy Glue

I took those vows, recited them, shaped my mouth around the vowels
like I was birthing them, like I was first to speak them.
I take you, to be my lawfully wedded . . .
And now, somehow, we are two roads diverged in a wood, full of travel and wear.
Me, me and you, I have tried to side-step onto the less-travelled,
Hoping you wouldn't notice me there.

The baby, the beautiful amazing baby,
is cooing right there on the living room floor.
We adore her, she knows she is adored, she is going to leave us behind
as she grows fully-evolved, one gorgeous opposable thumb.
We read to her and stare at her and gloss over each other's hair.
We have all the metaphors we need to call it quits,
as the glue between us crawls across the floor.

Blinded

Perhaps I suffer from oversight,
above the pale visible.
St. Francis blind through his weeping,
water smoothing his eyes to stone.
Water splashing and a clean echo in his mouth
like a wordless fairytale.
The visible world a cliff
to sail away from.
Mirrors unsilvering.
A Muslim bride full-face veiled,
so beautiful I cannot see you.
Your face is shining lightning in my hands.
My eyes settle into your memory.
My heart is beating,
my soul awake.
Joy rushing like an eternal waterfall.

Shore Leave

The mother smoothes out her face
to smooth away her son.
She lifts her labor
like her son could be lifted,
not up in her arms, but off.
Like she could deliver the years in two hands.

Her life is pierced and strung with him;
he's a knot she must undo.
Their roots tightly spooled and pulling.
She carried him for nothing,
then pushed.

He gulps milk,
smashes the empty bottle:
this is how a man treats his mother.
They wait on either side of the shards.

Lovely and Amazing

Leave it to the adopted child,
the expanding blackness in the family.
The girl eats and eats to swell her place.
She's unafraid of closing her mouth on the world.

One sister looks to every outside eye for examination.
This sister rescues stray dogs. She sees a stray in every mammal.
She deep down wishes for ugliness so she could win her own rescue.

The older sister dates her teenage boss.
He appreciates her handmade gift-wrap.
She wants to pull it away, rip away posters from the walls of his skin
and find a man.

The adopted girl fills herself with sugar and flour,
the best of a white world.
She takes her time adjusting each pillow for her mother
until each softness is perfectly placed, or rearranged.

I Remember High School

those days when I got the loving looks in the girls' bathroom,
the parking lot, the '78 Dodge backseat by chewing that watermelon
Bubblicious just enough to get the sugary spit on my lips,
its sweaty shine, and then take it, turn it, work it with my tongue
and blow it, make it a growing circle like small, small me
before it was me in my mama's belly, keep the slow breath moving
outwards so the bubble grows like Mama's belly
and without my permission, the gum has grown too thin
around my breath, now air, and it has broken, like my mama, deep in her belly,
wanted me to.

Self-Fertilization

She once waited on whims
of wind and insects.
Her brain like the sky:
a sheer cage exposed
to the wanderings of others.
Her body
a city spread out like loneliness.
The world
had been dreaming her
while she lay awake and still.
Now the clouds
are in heat, bringing the weather
down to her level.

She is an experimental animal
who yields herself.
Even before her
flowers open
she is breeding true
forming row and row of oat and seed.
The stimulation of her eye
and off springs
herself in a milk bottle.

Ribs radiating
and shimmering differently.

Now
with the exact opposite of altitude
she finds self-
compatibility.
Small inconspicuous flowers

which implode pure nerve.
Violent wings drawn inward
and pedalling faster.

She feels more like
herself.

The Child Inside Your Mind

Poetry reminds you of the child inside your mind.
The lesson of a children's story is—Tell me
a story about me.
And Mama complies—
here is a picture of a room
that could be your room,
here is a small baby,
here is a metallic page which reflects your infinitely-new face.
And this, too, is a poem's job—
here is a small story about everybody, about nobody,
and you.

In My Absence

My job is to make myself obsolete.
Even this poem is meant to replace me.
A mother's work is to create independence through love.
I am ending others' need of me.
When my toddler says, "Go that way, Mommy,"
I know I am winning.
I remain a memory inside her when elsewhere,
invisible as a heartbeat.
My death will be the height of my success,
when life replaces her sadness.

Acknowledgments

Grateful acknowledgment is made to the editors of the following publications, in which some of these poems appeared (or are quickly forthcoming), sometimes in different forms: *All We Can Hold: A Collection of Poetry on Motherhood*; Bigcitylit.com; *Chest Medical Journal*; The City Within (recording); *Grabbing the Apple: An Anthology of New York Women Poets*; hivhereandnow.com; *Hospital Drive*; *Lyre Lyre*; Mommikin.com; *Quail Bell Magazine*; *Remembering the Days That Breathed Pink*; *Slush Pile Magazine*; *Unshod Quills*; *The Vagina Project*; *WSQ: Women's Studies Quarterly*; and *Yes, Poetry*. Also kind thank you to Margaux Lange, partner in our online collaboration at http://ldyprts.tumblr.com, as well as to Lisa W. Rosenberg for hosting my work on her blog.

Thank you, thank you to Jessica Kristie and the devoted team at Winter Goose Publishing for bringing this decades-old dream into the world. It feels equal parts effort and miracle.

Thank you to my friends/teachers/muses whose nurturing, guidance, and criticism have sustained my words over the years, or years and years (in objectively alphabetical order): David Aglow, John M. Daley, Elaine Equi, Jennifer Faylor, Jane Gabriels, Sheila Maldonado, Quai Nystrom, David Pemberton, Melissa Petro and Gotham Writers Workshop, Jessica Rowshandel, Kimberly Shelby-Szyszko, Angelo Verga, Bakar Wilson, and Aaron Zimmerman and NY Writers Coalition, Inc. You are each so perfect at being you.

Thank you to my large and loving family: the Padnos-es, the Patsakos-es, the Fosters, and the ongoing weaving of lineages. To Daniel Shea, I knew you'd be a wonderful father, neither of us could glimpse how far you would exceed imagination.

To Mirabel Padnos Shea, I am convinced that the world will be better off with you in it. To my Mother, Evelyn Padnos, my original fearless woman. To my Father, Norman Padnos, the kindest man I've ever known. To Aunt Demi Kristy, who wears each day as a blessing.

Thank you for reading.

About the Author

Poet, social worker, mama, Scorpio, and suicide survivor are among the identities of Stella Padnos-Shea. Her poetry appears in various literary journals and forums, including *Women's Studies Quarterly*, *Mommikin*, and *Lady Parts*, a Barbie-themed collaboration with jewelry artist Margaux Lange. Stella currently works as a political organizer and therapist in New York City, but she has also embarked on her greatest and most challenging project yet: raising four-year-old daughter Mirabel with only hunches—at best—to go on.

www.ingramcontent.com/pod-product-compliance
Lightning Source LLC
Chambersburg PA
CBHW051347040426
42453CB00007B/457